Learn all the key facts with CGP!

Want to remember all the key information for AQA GCSE Business? This CGP Knowledge Organiser is here to help!

We've boiled down every topic to the important bits, with in-depth definitions and worked examples to cover everything you'll need.

There's also a matching Knowledge Retriever book that'll test you on every page — perfect for making sure you know it all!

CGP — still the best! ☺

Our sole aim here at CGP is to produce the highest quality books — carefully written, immaculately presented and dangerously close to being funny.

Then we work our socks off to get them out to you — at the cheapest possible prices.

Contents

Section 1 — Business in the Real World

Why Businesses Exist 2
Enterprise and Entrepreneurs 3
Business Ownership Structures 4
More Business Ownership Structures 5
Business Aims and Objectives 6
More on Business Objectives 7
Stakeholders 8
Resources 9
Revenue, Costs and Profit 10
The Business Plan 11
Location 12
Expanding Businesses 13
Internal Expansion 14
External Expansion 15

Section 2 — Influences on Business

Businesses and the Law 16
Technology and Business 17
Ethical Considerations 18
Environmental Influences 19
Businesses and the Economic Climate 20
Competition 21
Globalisation and Exchange Rates 22
Risks in Business 23

Section 3 — Business Operations

Supply Chains 24
More on Supply Chains 25
Production and Efficiency 26
Quality 27
Quality Management 28
Customer Service 29
More on Customer Service 30

Section 4 — Human Resources

Internal Organisational Structures 31
More on Organisational Structures 32
Contracts of Employment 33
Recruitment 34
Staff Training 35
Financial Motivation 36
Non-Financial Motivation 37

Section 5 — Marketing

The Marketing Mix...38
Market Research..39
More on Market Research..............................40
Product Life Cycles..41
Extension Strategies...42
Product Portfolios...43
Product Development..44
Price...45
Pricing Strategies..46
Methods of Promotion......................................47
More Methods of Promotion........................48
Place..49
E-Commerce..50

Section 6 — Finance

Sources of Finance...51
More Sources of Finance.................................52
Investments...53
Break-Even Analysis...54
More on Break-Even Analysis......................55
Cash Flow...56
More on Cash Flow...57
Income Statements...58
Profit Margins...59
Statements of Financial Position................60
More on Statements of
   Financial Position..61
Analysis of Financial Statements................62

Published by CGP.
Based on the classic CGP style created by Richard Parsons.

Editors: Molly Barker, Liam Dyer, Katherine Faudemer and Jack Simm.
Contributor: Colin Harber-Stuart.

With thanks to Michael Bushell and Judith Hayes for the proofreading.
With thanks to Hannah Wilkie for the copyright research.

ISBN: 978 1 83774 014 7

Printed by Elanders Ltd, Newcastle upon Tyne.
Clipart from Corel®

Text, design, layout and original illustrations © Coordination Group Publications Ltd (CGP) 2024
All rights reserved.

Photocopying more than one section of this book is not permitted, even if you have a CLA licence.
Extra copies are available from CGP with next day delivery. • 0800 1712 712 • www.cgpbooks.co.uk

Section 1 — Business in the Real World

Why Businesses Exist

Purpose of Businesses

Businesses sell products to customers.
Products can be goods or services.

GOOD	An item, e.g. a chocolate bar or an e-book
SERVICE	An action performed by other people to aid the customer, e.g. hairdressing.

Needs vs Wants

Goods or services can be:

1) **Needs** — things you can't live without.

2) **Wants** — things you'd like to have but can survive without.

Five Reasons for Starting a Business

1) To produce goods.
2) To provide a service.
3) To distribute goods to other businesses or individual customers.
4) To fulfil a business opportunity.
5) To benefit others. *This might be by making goods or providing a service.*

Three Sectors of the Economy

Sector of Economy	What it Does	Example of Business
1) PRIMARY	Produces raw materials for making goods or services. Raw materials can be: • extracted from the ground • grown • collected	• Mining industry • Farming industry • Fishing industry
2) SECONDARY	Manufactures goods.	• Food factories • Construction industry
3) TERTIARY	Provides services. Services can be for other businesses or consumers.	• Advertising industry • Shops • Restaurants • Banks

Enterprise and Entrepreneurs

Enterprise

ENTERPRISE — the process of identifying new business opportunities and taking advantage of them.

> Enterprise can involve starting a new business or expanding an existing one.

Four Qualities of Entrepreneurs

ENTREPRENEUR — someone who takes on the risks of enterprise activity.

An entrepreneur should be:

1. Hardworking
Long hours and lots of different tasks (e.g. accounting, business planning, sales and marketing).

2. Innovative
To come up with ideas and solve problems.

3. Organised
Need to keep on top of day-to-day tasks as well as planning for the future.

4. Willing to take risks
Running a business involves unknowns.
May need to give up current job and will need to invest money.

Six Objectives of Entrepreneurs

Reasons why someone might decide to be an entrepreneur:

1. Financial reasons
successful business → profit → earn more money

2. Gap in the market identified — sell a good or service no other business provides.

3. Be their own boss — make own decisions about business.

4. Flexible working hours — work around commitments.

5. Following an interest
interested in what they do → job satisfaction

6. Dissatisfaction with current job
new business → happier, more motivated

Section 1 — Business in the Real World

Business Ownership Structures

Unlimited vs Limited Liability

UNLIMITED LIABILITY — business owners are legally responsible for paying back all debts if the business fails (even if they have to sell everything they own).

LIMITED LIABILITY — business is legally responsible for paying back debts, not the owners. They only risk losing the money they have invested.

Legal Identities

INCORPORATED — the business has a separate legal identity from its owners. Any money, property, bills, etc. belong to the business not the owners.

UNINCORPORATED — the business has no legal identity. Suing the business means suing the owners.

Sole Traders

SOLE TRADER — a business with just one owner. (They can have other employees.)

Most small businesses, e.g. plumbers, hairdressers.

Tia was proud to be a local sole trader.

+ Advantages
- easy to set up
- full control over business and profit

— Disadvantages
- unlimited liability
- unincorporated
- responsibility can mean long hours and few holidays
- hard to raise money
  Banks see sole traders as risky.

Partnerships

E.g. solicitors, doctors' surgeries.

PARTNERSHIP — a business owned by a group of partners. Partners usually have an equal say in the business and equal shares of the profits.

+ Advantages
more owners means more...
- ideas
- skills
- capital (money)
- people to share work

— Disadvantages
- unlimited liability (usually)
- each partner is legally responsible for what all the others do
- partners have to share profits
- partners might disagree on business decisions

Section 1 — Business in the Real World

More Business Ownership Structures

Private Limited Companies

Owned by shareholders.
Shares can only be sold when all shareholders agree.

Private limited companies have 'Ltd.' after their name.

➕ Advantages
- limited liability
- incorporated
- easier to get loans

➖ Disadvantages
- expensive to set up
- required to publish accounts every year

Public Limited Companies

Owned by shareholders.
Company shares traded on stock exchange and can be bought and sold by anyone.

Public limited companies have 'PLC' after their name.

➕ Advantages
- limited liability
- incorporated
- more capital can be raised
- easy to expand and diversify

➖ Disadvantages
- lots of shareholders — hard to agree, and profit shared between more people
- possible for one person to buy enough shares to take over the company
- accounts are public, so competitors can see if business is struggling

Not-for-Profit Organisations

Don't try to make a profit:
- generate income to cover costs
- surplus put back into the business or used for community projects

➕ Advantages
- can have charitable status = tax relief
- can be eligible for grants

➖ Disadvantages
- can be hard to set up due to rules
- dependent on donations and grants
- can be hard to manage
- may rely on volunteers

Can choose to be:

1 An unincorporated association.
Easy to set up but the people involved have unlimited liability.

2 Incorporated.
Limited liability for people involved.
Often 'limited by guarantee' — members agree to pay a fixed amount if the business goes bust.

> Social enterprises are a type of not-for-profit that make money selling products but use the profit to benefit society.

Section 1 — Business in the Real World

Business Aims and Objectives

Aims

AIM — an overall goal that a business wants to achieve.

Once a firm knows its aims, it needs to set objectives.

Objectives

1. act as **measurable** steps on the way to an aim
2. act as **targets** for firms to work towards
3. can be used to measure whether a firm has been **successful**

E.g. Aim = growth
Objective = increase income from sales by 30% over two years.

Seven Business Aims

1. **Maximise profit** — this is an aim for almost all firms.

2. **Survival** — having enough money to stay open, e.g. to pay staff and buy stock to sell.

3. **Growth** — could be increasing:
   - employees
   - products sold
   - sales income

   Growth can be:
   - domestic (in the same country)
   - international (expand into other countries)

4. **Increase market share** — take sales from competitors or bring in new customers.

5. **Do what's right** — acting in ways that are best for society and are ethical.

6. **Increase shareholder value** — making shareholders more wealthy by increasing the value of the firm.

7. **Customer satisfaction** — when customers are happy with the product. Can be measured by market research.

Section 1 — Business in the Real World

More on Business Objectives

Factors Affecting Objectives

Size and age
Small or new firms often focus on customer satisfaction.

Bigger firms may focus on the environment and acting ethically.

Competition
Firms with lots of competition often focus on customer satisfaction and market share.

Firms with little competition can focus on profits and growth.

Type of business
Not-for-profit firms may focus on social and ethical objectives and less on profit or growth.

Ways Objectives Change

As a firm grows and evolves, its objectives are likely to change.

New start-up
→ focus on survival

Stable business
→ focus on growth and maximising profits

Large established business
→ focus on having largest market share and expansion into other countries

May become public limited company
→ focus on increasing shareholder value

Changes in Business Environment

Businesses react to external changes by changing their objectives:

1) Changes in technology
- New technology is more efficient.
- Firms spend more money on equipment and training than growth.

2) New legislation
- New laws affect a firm's costs.
- Firms adapt to meet new rules, e.g. paying staff higher wages.

3) Economic changes
- In a recession, growth objectives are put on hold.
- Firm concentrates on survival.

4) Environmental expectations
- Many customers are concerned about environmental impact.
- Firms change their environmental objectives to keep customers.

Section 1 — Business in the Real World

Stakeholders

Influence of Stakeholders

STAKEHOLDER — anyone who's affected by a business.

Businesses are also affected by stakeholders, as their opinions must be considered when setting objectives.

Different stakeholders can have *conflicting opinions*, so businesses need to decide who to listen to in each situation.

When selling hiking gear, it's important to keep your stickholders happy.

Six Examples of Stakeholders

Shareholders get paid dividends when the firm makes profit.

Stakeholders	Like objectives based on...	Reason
1. Owners / shareholders	Profitability and growth	They get more money.
2. Employees	Profitability and growth	Better job security and career prospects.
	Ethics	Better wages and working conditions.
3. Suppliers	Profitability and growth	They get more custom.
4. Local community	Profitability and growth	May provide new jobs and mean people have more money to spend in local shops. Local activities may be sponsored.
	Ethics and the environment	Local environment isn't harmed, e.g. by noise or air pollution.
5. Government	Profitability, growth and job creation	More money from taxes.
6. Customers	Customer satisfaction	High quality products and low prices.

Section 1 — Business in the Real World

Resources

Four Factors of Production

① LAND — actual 'territory' and all Earth's natural resources.
- **Non-renewable resources**
  E.g. oil, coal
- **Renewable resources**
  E.g. tidal power, wood
- **Mined materials**
  E.g. gold
- **Water**
- **Animals**

Nearly all resources classed as land are scarce.

Capital has to be made — it isn't a natural resource.

② CAPITAL — equipment, factories and schools needed to produce goods or services.

③ LABOUR — work done by people during the production process.

Different levels of education, experience and training make some people more productive.

④ ENTERPRISE — entrepreneurs creating products from the other factors of production.

Providing these factors can be rewarded with wages, rent, interest or profit.

Opportunity Costs

OPPORTUNITY COST — the value of the next best alternative that's been given up.

- Most factors of production are limited.
- Money or time spent doing one thing means missing out on doing other things.
- Opportunity cost puts a value on a business decision in terms of what is given up.
- Businesses can compare opportunity costs to decide the best way to use resources.

Section 1 — Business in the Real World

Revenue, Costs and Profit

Revenue

REVENUE — income businesses make by selling products.

sales = number of units sold

revenue = sales × price

EXAMPLE
The stationery company Jot It Down sells 10 000 notebooks for £5 each. What is their sales revenue?

revenue = 10 000 × £5 = £50 000

Costs

FIXED COSTS — costs that don't change with output, e.g. rent, insurance, advertising.

Fixed costs are paid even if the business produces nothing.

Fixed costs are only fixed in the short term — they increase as the business grows.

VARIABLE COSTS — costs that increase as output increases, e.g. factory labour, raw materials, running machinery.

The total cost is the sum of the fixed costs and variable costs.

total cost = total fixed cost + total variable cost

Average Unit Cost

- Average unit cost is how much each product costs to make.

Average unit costs usually fall as a firm grows.

average unit cost = total cost ÷ output

number of products made

EXAMPLE
The total cost for Jot It Down to produce 3000 calculators is £9000. What is the average unit cost?

average unit cost = £9000 ÷ 3000 = £3

- To make a profit, the firm must charge a higher price than the average unit cost.

Profit and Loss

PROFIT — the difference between revenue and costs over a period of time.

profit = revenue − costs

If costs are higher than revenue, the business makes a loss — the amount of profit is negative.

EXAMPLE
In May, Jot It Down has a revenue of £10 000, and has total costs of £4000. How much profit does Jot It Down make in May?

profit = £10 000 − £4000
= £6000

Section 1 — Business in the Real World

The Business Plan

Four Reasons for Business Plans

BUSINESS PLAN — an outline of what a business will do and how it will do it.

They can be used to plan new businesses or make changes to existing businesses.

1. Forces owner to think carefully about the business's purpose, organisation and necessary resources.
   → Owner can work out how much money is needed.

2. Convinces financial backers that it's a good investment.

3. Identifies if it's a bad idea early on — before time and money are wasted.

4. Helps to decide objectives needed to achieve the business's aims.

Sections of Business Plans

Usually also an executive summary at the start that outlines the whole thing.

BUSINESS PLAN: Geraldine's Ices

Personal details of owner and any key personnel, e.g. their CVs.

Mission statement — describes the broad aims of the business, e.g. to become market leader in their sector.

Objectives are more specific than aims, e.g. a sales target.

Product Description — including marketing strategy and how the unique selling point will be achieved.

Production details — how the product is made or the service is provided, including equipment needed and location.

Staffing requirements — number of staff, their job descriptions, expected wage bill.

Finance — money needed to start the business and forecasts for things like cash flow, profit, return on investment.

Three Drawbacks of Business Plans

1. Plans take time and money to write. → The benefit may not outweigh the cost.

2. The plan may be too optimistic. → If sales are lower than predicted, the business may struggle to pay its bills.

3. Firms may stick too tightly to the plan. → Not adapting the plan for unexpected changes can cause problems.

Section 1 — Business in the Real World

Location

Raw Materials

Locating near to raw materials means lower transport costs.

E.g. a jam manufacturer may locate near a farm or orchard.

Labour Supply

- Areas with high unemployment have lower wages and good labour supply.
- Towns and cities might have colleges that can provide training.

Market Location

Locating near customers has benefits:

1 Cheaper to transport finished product if customers are nearby.

Businesses that trade over the internet can be more flexible about their location.

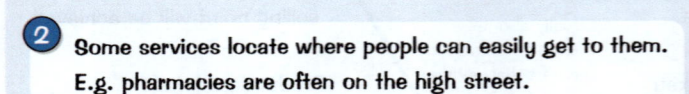

2 Some services locate where people can easily get to them.
E.g. pharmacies are often on the high street.

Mandy wished she sold snorkels, not skis.

3 Global firms may set up their production in countries with a large market.
- Reduces transport costs.
- No import taxes.

Cost

- **Cost of labour varies between countries.**
  E.g. large firms often have factories in India or China where wages are lower.
- **Price of renting or buying premises varies between different areas.**
  E.g. high street premises are more expensive than an industrial park.
- **Governments might give grants or tax breaks to firms located in areas of high unemployment.**

Competition

Being near competitors has advantages and disadvantages.

➕ Advantages
- Easy to find skilled labour
- Existing local suppliers
- Customers know where to come

➖ Disadvantage
Loss of sales to competitors

Section 1 — Business in the Real World

Expanding Businesses

Economies of Scale

Bigger firms make more products and have more money. This can lead to economies of scale.

ECONOMY OF SCALE — when there is a reduction in average unit costs due to producing on a large scale.

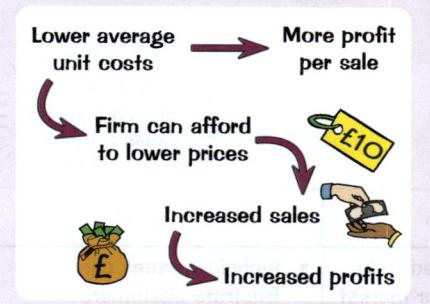

Lower average unit costs → More profit per sale
↓
Firm can afford to lower prices
↓
Increased sales
↓
Increased profits

Increase in profit due to economies of scale can fund further expansion.

Purchasing Economies of Scale

Firm buys supplies in bulk.
↳ Cheaper unit price.
  ↳ Lower average unit cost.

Technical Economies of Scale

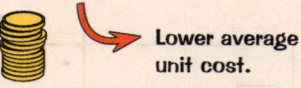

- Bigger firms can afford to buy and operate more advanced machinery.
  ↳ Machinery is more efficient to run.
    ↳ Lower average unit cost.
- Bigger firms often have larger premises.
  ↳ Cheaper per unit area than smaller premises.

E.g. a factory that is 10 times bigger is less than 10 times as expensive.

This is the law of increased dimensions.

Diseconomies of Scale

DISECONOMY OF SCALE — an increase in average unit costs due to a business being larger.

Reasons for diseconomies of scale:

1 Management
Bigger businesses are harder and more expensive to manage.

2 Production
Production processes are usually more complex and difficult to organise for larger firms.

3 Employees
Larger firms have more people, so harder to communicate.
- Takes time for decisions to reach workforce.
- Employees at bottom of organisational structure can feel insignificant.
- Workers can be demotivated, lowering productivity.

Section 1 — Business in the Real World

Internal Expansion

Advantages and Disadvantages of Internal Expansion

INTERNAL EXPANSION — when a business grows by expanding its own activities.

+ Advantages
- fairly inexpensive
- low risk
- slower pace of growth makes it easier to maintain quality and train staff

Internal expansion generally involves a firm doing more of what it's already good at.

− Disadvantage
takes a long time to achieve growth

Internal expansion can also be called organic growth.

Methods of Internal Expansion

		+ Advantages	**− Disadvantages**
	Selling online	• customers don't need to be near a shop — larger market • no rent and fewer staff needed than a physical store	• technical issues can frustrate customers • technology needs regular updates
	Opening new stores	• low risk — likely a success if similar to existing stores	• extra costs, e.g. rent, staff pay
	Outsourcing — paying another firm to carry out tasks that could be done internally.	Tasks might be done... • faster • cheaper • to a better standard	• less control • outsourcing firm has other customers and priorities • standards of outsourcing firm will affect reputation

Franchising

FRANCHISING — one firm lets other firms sell its products (or use its trademarks) in return for a fee or percentage of profits.

- The product manufacturer is a *franchisor*.
- A firm selling the franchisor's products is a *franchisee*.

+
- increased income for franchisor
- more market share and brand awareness
- franchisee responsible for the risks and costs of running a new outlet

− brand can get a bad reputation if the franchisee has poor standards

Section 1 — Business in the Real World

External Expansion

Mergers and Takeovers

Two ways of achieving external expansion:

1. **MERGER** — two firms join together to form a new, larger firm.
2. **TAKEOVER** — an existing firm expands by buying more than half the shares in another firm.

➕ External expansion means the business grows much more quickly than with internal expansion.

The Stone May & Sons takeover of Tee Time went to plan.

Four Ways Mergers or Takeovers Happen

1. Firm joins with a **supplier**.

   ➕ Firm controls the supply, cost and quality of its raw materials.

2. Firm takes over one of its **customers**.

   E.g. a manufacturer takes over a chain of retail outlets.

   ➕ Firm has greater access to the market.

3. A firm joins with one of its **competitors**.

   ➕ Firm has more economies of scale and gets a bigger market share. So it's a stronger competitor.

4. Two **unrelated firms** join.

   ➕ Firm diversifies into new markets, reducing risk from relying on few products.

Problems with Mergers and Takeovers

- Can create bad feeling — some takeovers are hostile and unpopular.
- Hard to make two different businesses work as one. ➡ Management style or culture might differ. This can lead to unmotivated employees.
- Can lead to cost-cutting. ➡ This might involve redundancies, leading to tension and uncertainty among workers.

Most takeovers and mergers are unsuccessful.

Section 1 — Business in the Real World

Section 2 — Influences on Business

Businesses and the Law

Pay

There's a minimum amount that firms need to pay their workers:
- **National Minimum Wage** — for workers aged 20 and under, of school leaving age.
- **National Living Wage** — for workers aged 21 and over.

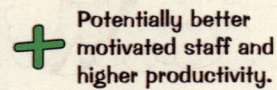

+ Potentially better motivated staff and higher productivity.

− Can increase business costs, meaning: higher prices → reduced sales → reduced income

Discrimination

Equality Act (2010) — employers can't discriminate against anyone because of:

race   sexual orientation   age
religion   disabilities   gender

This affects recruitment and pay — staff must be paid the same for doing the same job, or work of equal value.

Firms write policies and train staff about discrimination issues.

Health and Safety

Health and Safety at Work Act (1974) — firms must:
- carry out risk assessments to identify workplace dangers.
- take reasonable steps to reduce risks.
- provide staff with health and safety training and suitable equipment.

+ Reduces staff injuries, so a more productive workforce.

− Higher costs for businesses (e.g. paying for training courses).

Consumer Law

Consumer Rights Act 2015 — covers how products can be sold.

Three criteria a product must meet:

1 **Be fit for purpose** — it has to do the job it was designed for.

2 **Match its description** — it must match how the business describes it (trade description), e.g. size, quantity, materials.
It's illegal to falsely claim it's endorsed by a person or organisation.

3 **Be of satisfactory quality** — it should be well made and shouldn't cause problems for the buyer.

Impacts of Breaking Laws

Consumer law:
- Customers can ask for a *refund, repair* or *replacement*.
- Customers could take the business to *court*, which can be very costly.
- The business could get a *bad reputation*, which could reduce sales.

Employment law:
- Compensation costs
- Fines
- Bad publicity
- Closure of the firm

Technology and Business

Impact of Changing Technology

ICT includes things such as computers, phone networks and the internet.

+
- Computers can do jobs more quickly.
- People can communicate more easily. → Reduced long-term costs — fewer work-hours are needed to do tasks.

−
- New equipment is expensive to buy.
- Staff need to be hired or trained to use new technology.

E-Commerce

E-COMMERCE — buying and selling products using the internet.

+ Good for firms as they can reach wider markets.

Firms need to adapt to the growing need to use e-commerce by e.g.:
- building websites,
- employing IT specialists,
- developing ways to distribute to online customers.

Six Methods of Digital Communication

1 Websites — Useful for a wide range of stakeholders. E.g. can provide product information for customers and publish reports for shareholders.

2 Apps — Used to sell products and communicate with customers, e.g. about promotions.

3 Social media — Good way to communicate with a large group of people. Used for customer service and promotion, e.g. to advertise products or events.

4 Email — Quick and easy way to communicate either with individuals or a larger group of people.

5 Video calls — Convenient way to have meetings with stakeholders based in different locations, e.g. employees on different sites.

6 Live chats — Instant messages often used for customer service and communication between employees.

Section 2 — Influences on Business

Ethical Considerations

Acting Ethically

ETHICS — the moral principles of right and wrong.
Ethical issues are important, so many businesses try to act ethically.

Overseas employees
Firms can write codes of conduct to limit the number of hours for workers in overseas factories.

In some countries, it's not illegal for people to work long hours for low pay.

UK employees
Firms can:
- pay staff fairly
- keep personal details safe
- provide a comfortable working environment

Buying raw materials
Firms can buy raw materials from **Fairtrade** sources, so workers from developing countries earn better wages.

Promoting products
Firms follow codes of practice to not criticise other brands. Some products can't be advertised at all, e.g. cigarettes.

Product development
Firms can choose non-toxic materials for their products and not test on animals.

Balancing Ethics and Profit

Businesses have their own **ethical policies** — these are ways of working that stakeholders think are fair and honest.

But there's a **trade-off** between acting ethically and making the most profit.

Advantages of acting ethically
- can be used to promote products
- can attract new customers
- appeals to shareholders/investors
- staff more motivated and productive

Disadvantages of acting ethically
- expensive — firms may have to pay more for staff and materials
- may be hard to find ethical suppliers
- lower profit per product sold

Section 2 — Influences on Business

Environmental Influences

Five Ways to Reduce Environmental Impacts

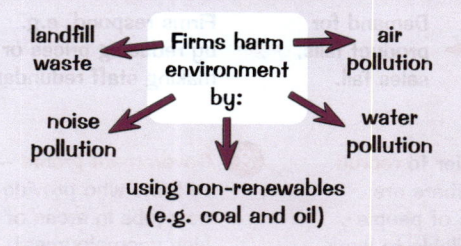

Firms harm environment by:
- landfill waste
- air pollution
- noise pollution
- water pollution
- using non-renewables (e.g. coal and oil)

1. use less packaging
2. recycle unwanted goods
3. dispose of waste responsibly
4. encourage car share schemes or cycling to work
5. buy quieter machinery or use insulation

Global Impact of Business

The combined impact of global businesses is damaging the Earth.

Many industries and power stations release carbon dioxide — which contributes to global warming.

Global warming has knock-on effects for plant and animal life.

More carbon dioxide in atmosphere → Climate becomes warmer → Ice caps melt — sea levels rise, more flooding

Sustainable Business

Many firms want to be more sustainable — working in a way to not damage the Earth for future generations, e.g.:

- using renewable energy resources
- using less-polluting vehicles and machinery
- using more efficient electrical goods

+ Advantages
- appeals to customers interested in being environmentally friendly
- can give competitive advantage

− Disadvantage
more sustainable processes and new equipment can be expensive — this may lead to lower profits

Section 2 — Influences on Business

Businesses and the Economic Climate

Unemployment

Lots of people unemployed. → People have less money to spend. → Demand for product falls, sales fall. → Firms respond, e.g. by reducing prices or making staff redundant.

But there are potential **benefits**:

1) Less money spent on **wages** — people may be prepared to work for less money.

2) Easier to **recruit** — there are lots of people available to work.

3) **Government grants** — to firms who provide new jobs in areas of high unemployment.

Consumer Income

The amount consumers earn increases over time.

Businesses that sell things at discount prices might benefit as more people try to spend less.

If prices rise at a **faster rate** than income... → Greater proportion of people's income spent on essential items, e.g. food.

When this happens, income is going down in 'real terms'.

Less money available for luxuries, e.g. holidays, so demand for these decreases.

Businesses selling luxuries see fall in sales and profits.

The **opposite** is true when income rises at a **faster rate** than prices rise.

Interest Rate Changes

INTEREST RATE — a percentage that shows the cost of borrowing money or the reward given for saving money.

Amount needing to be paid back on existing borrowed money may also fall.

If interest rate is cut...
↓
Cheaper to borrow money. Less money made on savings.

Lower interest rates **Increased** spending %↓

Higher interest rates **Decreased** spending %↑

Consumers borrow more and save less. They have more money to spend.
↓
Demand for products goes up.
↓
Sales and profits increase.

Businesses borrow more. They have more money to invest in the business.
↓
Increased investment leads to growth.

The **opposite** is true when interest rates increase — demand for products goes down, and businesses have less money. This may lead to slower growth and cost-cutting.

Section 2 — Influences on Business

Competition

Markets

The word market can mean:

1. a place where goods are traded.
2. trade in a particular type of product.
3. the potential customers for a product.

Competitive Markets

COMPETITOR — a business that sells the same products in the same market as another business.

Competitive markets have many competitors — a large number of producers selling to a large number of consumers.

Effects on a business in a competitive market:

- Can't dictate prices — charging too much will mean consumers go elsewhere.
  - So firms have to make production efficient.

- Customers need convincing — firms have to persuade customers that their product is better than their rivals'.
  - So firms spend more on, e.g. promotions and developing high quality products.

- Firms look to fill any gaps in the market.
  - So firms spend lots on developing new products.

Lots of competition means firms often make the exact same product.

Competition only over product's selling price. → Prices and profits driven down. → Less money to develop new, better products.

Three Markets with Minimal Competition

1. When a firm launches a brand new product, there won't be any competition. If consumers want the product, they have to buy from this firm.

2. Specialist products will have low competition. The market won't be big enough for many businesses to survive.

3. Some markets are too expensive to start a business in. There will be low competition as few businesses can afford the cost.

Ori tried to enter the airline indutry, but the costs were sky-high.

Section 2 — Influences on Business

Globalisation and Exchange Rates

International Trade

GLOBALISATION — the process by which businesses and countries around the world become more connected.

Import = buying goods from abroad. Export = selling goods abroad.

UK businesses compete internationally by:

- investing in the design of new products or processes.
- maintaining high quality standards, while keeping prices lower than competitors.

Effects of Globalisation

Advantages
- larger market means increased sales and cheaper supplies
- setting up factories near raw materials reduces transport costs and import taxes
- labour can be cheaper overseas

Disadvantages
- average UK wage is high, so hard to compete with other countries
- potential of bad publicity if seen to be exploiting workers overseas
- profits can be affected by changes in exchange rate

Exchange Rate Basics

EXCHANGE RATE — the price at which one currency can be traded for another.

Exchange rates fluctuate — they are affected by the economy of the country that uses the currency, and by the global economy.

Value of the Pound

Fall in £ value — good for exporters
- UK products sold abroad get cheaper to buy abroad. → Increased sales and profits for firms that export a lot.
- Foreign products sold in the UK get more expensive. → Costs increase for UK firms importing raw materials. → May need to increase prices. Profits may fall.

Rise in £ value — good for importers
- UK products sold abroad get more expensive to buy abroad. → Decreased sales and profits for firms that export a lot.
- Foreign products sold in the UK get cheaper. → Costs decrease for UK firms importing raw materials. → Profits may rise.

Section 2 — Influences on Business

Risks in Business

Three Risks for Businesses

All businesses face risks and uncertainties:

1. Starting a business

- Entrepreneurs need money for equipment and staff.
- They may use their own money and borrow from banks and investors.
- Profits must be made to pay back money owed or the firm will fail.

2. Health of the economy

- Affects unemployment levels, interest rates and exchange rates.
- Changes can affect demand for products and investment in a business.

3. Actions of competitors

- Competitors may bring out new products.
- Firms may struggle if they lose market share to competitors.

Planning to Reduce Risk

- Do a proper business plan.
- Make plans in order to change or grow the business.
- Have plan Bs in place for different scenarios, e.g. what to do if a supplier goes bust.

Eh, looks clear.

If only pheasants would weigh up their risks more often...

Researching to Reduce Risk

Research helps businesses prepare for changes and put plans in place for dealing with them.

- Carry out regular market research — to check the marketing mix is right for their products.
- Research the competition — to be aware of new competitors, products and pricing changes.
- Research predicted changes to the economy — e.g. from planned changes to the law.

Section 2 — Influences on Business

Section 3 — Business Operations

Supply Chains

Supply Chain Basics

SUPPLY CHAIN — the group of firms that are involved in the processes required to make a finished product or service available to the customer.

The supply chain will vary depending on the product or service, but will typically be:

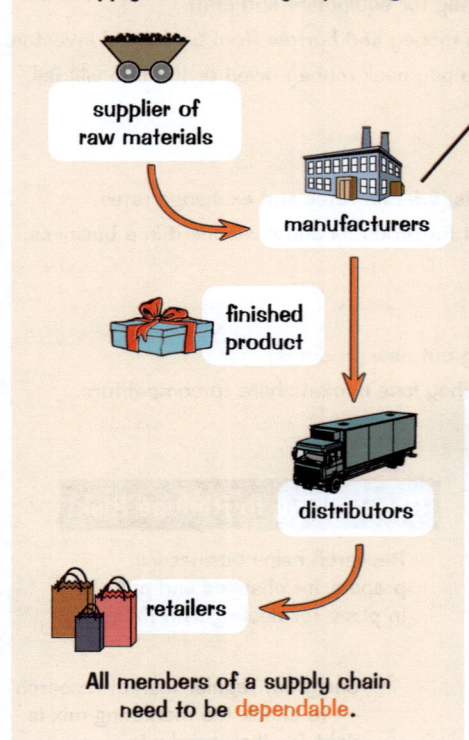

- supplier of raw materials
- manufacturers
- finished product
- distributors
- retailers

Some of these steps could be skipped, e.g. a distributor might take products straight to the consumer.

Distributor — buys products from a manufacturer and sells them to businesses and consumers.
Retailer — sells products directly to consumers.

All members of a supply chain need to be **dependable**.

Choosing a Supplier

Three things to consider:

1) Cost

Cheaper suppliers might have lower quality products. It might be better to pay more to get, e.g. better quality products or faster delivery.

2) Quality

Quality needs to be consistent.
Customers may blame firms over suppliers for poor quality products and choose to shop elsewhere.

3) Reliability

Delivery from suppliers should be reliable — goods should arrive on time and be high quality.

Section 3 — Business Operations

More on Supply Chains

Procurement and Logistics

PROCUREMENT — finding and buying things that a firm needs from suppliers outside of the firm.

LOGISTICS — getting goods or services from one part of the supply chain to another.

Two benefits of effective procurement and logistics systems:

1) Improved efficiency
- The business gets the supplies it needs at the right time.
- This means there are no breaks in production and no materials are wasted.

2) Reduced costs
- The business gets supplies at the best price (so money is not wasted).
- This reduces unit costs, so the firm can make more profit on each item, or reduce prices.

Three Reasons for Managing a Supply Chain Effectively

1) Develops good relationships
Businesses that work closely with suppliers can carry out processes in efficient and cost-effective ways.

2) Gets the best price and value
There can be many suppliers for a business to choose from.

Businesses that research suppliers can get the best price and value for the goods they need.

3) Reduces waste and unnecessary costs
Businesses should reduce waste and cut unnecessary costs in their supply chain.

This helps to make the business more streamlined and have faster production times.

Section 3 — Business Operations

Production and Efficiency

Job Production

JOB PRODUCTION — each product has a unique design based on the customer's specification.

+
- Unique, high-quality products — customers are willing to pay a high price, which can lead to higher profits.

−
- High labour costs for skilled, highly-paid workers.
- Often expensive and time-consuming.

Flow Production

FLOW PRODUCTION — products are identical and made as quickly as possible. Production is continuous.

+
- Gain from economies of scale — low unit costs means low, competitive prices.
- High productivity.

−
- Capital-intensive — lots of money is needed initially, e.g. to buy machinery.
- Lots of space usually needed, e.g. to store products.

Lean Production

LEAN PRODUCTION — the business aims to use as few resources and to have as little waste as possible.

JUST-IN-TIME (JIT) — a form of lean production where products are made just in time for delivery to customers.

Two Ways to Manage Stock

1 **JUST-IN-TIME (JIT)** — stock levels are kept at a bare minimum.

+
- Less money spent storing stock, e.g. on warehouse space and staff.

−
- More cost for frequent stock deliveries.
- Less gain from economies of scale — stock isn't bought in bulk.

2 **JUST-IN-CASE (JIC)** — buffer stocks are kept at every stage of the process in case of a supply shortage or an increase in customer demand.

+
- Production can continue if there's a problem with deliveries of raw materials.

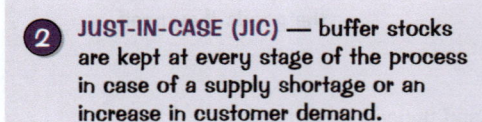

−
- Can be costly storing extra stock.

'Stock' can mean any item that's needed in production or distribution, e.g. raw materials or a finished product.

Section 3 — Business Operations

Quality

Customer Expectations

Customers expect quality from all parts of a business:

Goods
- Customers expect products to be of good quality.
- They should work properly and not break.

Services
- Services should be of good quality.
  E.g. a bus company needs to make sure its buses are clean, well-maintained and on time.
- Customers also expect a high standard of customer service.

Three Benefits of Maintaining Quality

1. Higher price
Customers will often pay a higher price for better quality products.

2. Increased sales
Customers who are happy with quality are more likely to make repeat purchases, which increases sales.

3. Better reputation
Businesses that provide high quality products will have a better reputation and image.
They'll gain new customers and existing customers are likely to use the business again.

Two Costs of Maintaining Quality

1. Staff training
Staff need to be able to do their job properly to produce high quality products.
Staff training costs time and money.

2. Inspection
Products need to be inspected to check their quality.
This costs time and money.

Two Costs of Not Maintaining Quality

1. Disrupted provision of services
A drop in quality can disrupt the services that a business offers.
This can mean a loss of sales.

2. Product recalls
Unsafe products are recalled. A refund or replacement would need to be offered.
This can be costly and can affect the firm's reputation.

Section 3 — Business Operations

Quality Management

Quality Checks

Firms check quality to find faults before products reach the customer. Firms usually check:

A firm needs to decide what level of quality is acceptable to them.

1. Raw materials from suppliers. → 2. Random samples of work in progress. → 3. Random samples of finished products.

Quality checks can be expensive, but still less costly than customers returning items or not buying from the firm again.

Three Ways to Measure Quality

1. Test the physical properties (e.g. size and colour) match the exact specifications.

2. Monitor how many returns and customer complaints there are.

   The firm can decide what level of returns or complaints it's comfortable with.

3. Do customer surveys to assess how satisfied customers are.

Total Quality Management (TQM)

TOTAL QUALITY MANAGEMENT — a strategy that aims to make every employee in a firm responsible for quality to ensure that it remains consistent.

The focus is on:

- Getting things right first time. This reduces costs by reducing waste.

- Increasing customer satisfaction — emphasis is put on the quality of production and after-sales service.

Maintaining Quality with Growth

business grows quickly → output of products needs to increase quickly → more difficult to keep quality standards high

- It may become hard to carry out all the necessary quality inspections.
- Corners may be cut to make products quicker.
- More employees may be needed — but it takes time to train new workers.

A growing business might:

- become a **franchisor** — but keeping high quality standards across the franchises can involve a lot of staff training and regular inspections.

- **outsource** some tasks — but it can be expensive to outsource to a firm that delivers high quality (and using a cheaper firm can lead to a fall in quality).

Section 3 — Business Operations

Customer Service

Providing Customer Service

CUSTOMER SERVICE — any interaction a business has with its customers.

Firms should provide great customer service throughout the sales process.

Three Ways of Providing Good Customer Service

1) Have excellent product knowledge
- Questions are answered quickly and accurately.
- Customer gets product most suited to their needs.
- Customer feels confident buying from the firm.

2) Engage well with customers
- Staff should be polite, friendly, listen to customer needs and create a positive atmosphere.
- Makes customer feel important and valued.
- Have extra ways of making the experience positive, e.g. free refreshments or next-day delivery.

3) Offer post-sales service
- Offer user training to customer on how to use product.
- Have a post-sales helpline where staff can help to resolve any issues.
- Offer servicing for products that require it.
  E.g. cars and boilers.

Dhruv thought it was probably about time for a post sales service.

Six Stages of the Sales Process

1. Finding new customers
2. Approaching the customer
3. Assessing their needs
4. Presenting products to them
5. Closing (customer agrees to buy)
6. Follow-up

Section 3 — Business Operations

More on Customer Service

Advances in Technology

Many customers now have easy access to the internet and choose to do things online. This has changed how firms provide customer service.

Websites and E-commerce

E-commerce is buying and selling products using the internet.

Websites can be used for e-commerce and providing good customer service.

Websites:
- allow 24-hour ordering.
- provide ways of contacting the firm.
- allow access to services via online accounts.

Social Media

Social media allows communication and the sharing of content online.

Social media can be used:
- by firms to communicate with customers (e.g. to show them how to use a product).
- by customers to contact a firm (e.g. with queries or complaints).

Importance of Good Customer Service

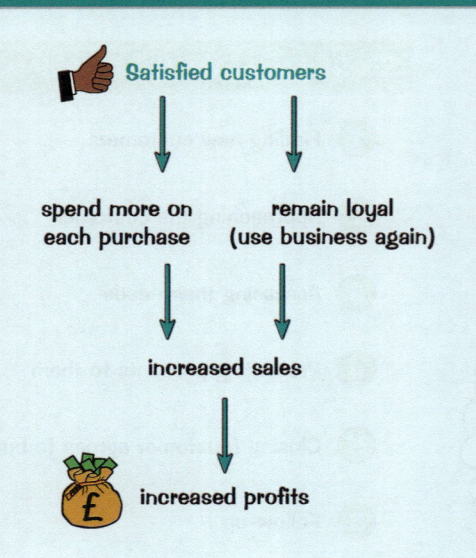

For many firms, providing good customer service increases profitability, so the benefit outweighs the cost.

Satisfied customers
- spend more on each purchase
- remain loyal (use business again)
→ increased sales → increased profits

Dissatisfied customers
- tell others about bad experience
- don't use firm again
→ damaged brand image → reduced sales → reduced profits

Section 3 — Business Operations

Section 4 — Human Resources

Internal Organisational Structures

Four Layers within a Hierarchy

Reasons for internal organisational structures:
- individual responsibilities are clear
- a job role exists for every activity

1. **DIRECTORS** — responsible for the business's strategy.
2. **MANAGERS** — organise carrying out the strategy.
3. **SUPERVISORS** — look after specific projects or small teams of operatives.
4. **OPERATIVES** — given tasks by supervisors or managers.

At each level some responsibility is delegated to the level below.

SPAN OF CONTROL — number of workers reporting to one manager.

CHAIN OF COMMAND — chain connecting directors to operatives.

Tall Organisational Structure

- Long chain of command
- More layers of management 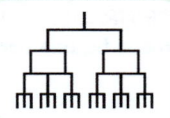
- Managers have narrow span of control

→ Workers can be monitored closely
→ Firm is more effective

Communication can be slow and difficult.
- Lots of people passing the message along chain of command.
- Verbal communication is hard if lots of managers need to be involved.

Flat Organisational Structure

- Short chain of command 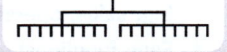
- Managers have a wide span of control

→ Can be difficult to effectively manage a lot of employees at once

Fast communication — few layers of management. E.g. via email or group meetings.
- Easy to pass on one message to everyone.
- Hard for managers to talk to each worker individually.

Changing Organisational Structures

Small firms have flat structures, often run by just the owner. → Firm grows →
1. Employs more staff.
2. Employs managers to organise workforce.
3. Structure gets taller.

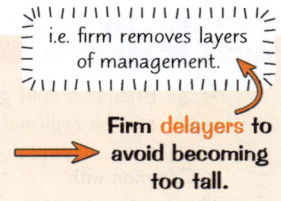

→ Firm **delayers** to avoid becoming too tall. (i.e. firm removes layers of management.)

More on Organisational Structures

Centralised vs Decentralised

CENTRALISED STRUCTURE — all major decisions made by one person or a few senior managers.

DECENTRALISED STRUCTURE — authority to make most decisions is shared out.

Decision makers
- (+) Senior managers are experienced, with an overview of whole firm.
- (−) May lack specialist knowledge or have lost their touch.
- (+) Employees have specialist knowledge.
- (−) They may not see overall needs of firm.

Reaction to change
- (−) Decision-making and communication takes longer — firm slow to react to change.
- (+) Changes might not need senior managers to approve, so they can be made quickly.

Consistency within firm
- (+) Policies uniform throughout firm.
- (−) Lack of consistency between departments or regions.

Businesses may decentralise as they grow.

Function-based Structure

- Business split into functional areas. E.g. sales, operations, human resources.
- Each functional area does one part of the business's work.

- (+) Specialists concentrate on their job.
- (−) Different departments might not work together well.

Common with limited companies.

Product-based Structure

Business split into different sectors according to the product made. E.g. food, books, toiletries.

Common with large manufacturers.

- (+) Managers make decisions relevant to product sector.
- (−) Wasteful duplication of resources between sectors.

Region-based Structure

Business split geographically — can be regional or national.

Common with multinational businesses.

- (+) Management spread out — day-to-day control easier.
- (−) Wasteful duplication of resources between regions.

Section 4 — Human Resources

Contracts of Employment

Information in Contracts

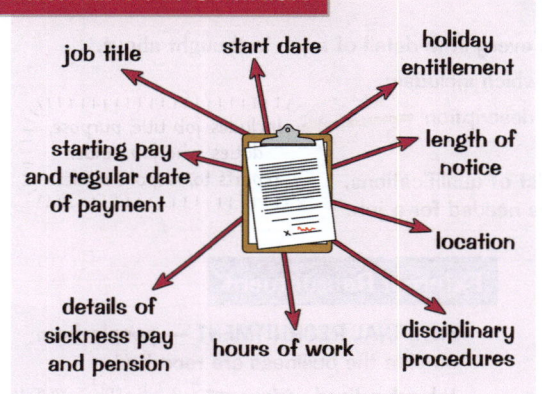

- job title
- start date
- holiday entitlement
- starting pay and regular date of payment
- length of notice
- location
- details of sickness pay and pension
- hours of work
- disciplinary procedures

Full-Time vs Part-Time

Full-time = about 35-40 hours a week.

Part-time = between 10-30 hours a week.

- Some people work full-time for financial reasons.
- Some people work part-time to spend extra time with family.

Kisi wished she'd read the job description properly.

Advantages of full-time employees	Advantages of part-time employees
Employees likely have only one job — so firms have more control over when they work.	• Employees often flexible with hours and can fill in for absent staff. • Good for firms that are only busy at certain periods.

Job Shares

Two employees share the work and pay of one full-time job.

Advantages

- Employees can work extra hours if the other is absent — full job still gets done.
- Employees bring different strengths to the job.
- Good for employees who want to work part-time hours.

For job shares to work, each employee's responsibilities must be clear and there must be good communication.

Zero Hour Contracts

A zero hour contract means:
- employer doesn't have to offer any work
- employee doesn't have to accept any work

Used in businesses with lots of fluctuations in demand. — E.g. restaurants, hotels.

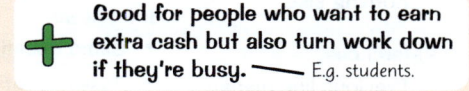

- Firms don't waste money paying staff when they aren't needed — cheap form of labour.
- Good for people who want to earn extra cash but also turn work down if they're busy. — E.g. students.
- Can be hard for people who rely on the work to earn a living.

Section 4 — Human Resources

Recruitment

Two Features of Job Adverts

JOB ANALYSIS — process in which every little detail of a job is thought about.
This is used to create a job advert which includes:

1. **JOB DESCRIPTION** — written description of what a job involves. → *Includes: job title, purpose, duties, who job holder reports to, responsibilities.*
2. **PERSON SPECIFICATION** — list of qualifications, skills, experience and attitudes needed for a job.

Internal Recruitment

INTERNAL RECRUITMENT — existing employees are recruited into new roles within a business. Job advertised within the business.

+
- cheaper to recruit
- posts filled quickly
- candidates already know firm, managers already know candidates

−
- fewer new ideas
- candidate's previous role must be filled

External Recruitment

EXTERNAL RECRUITMENT — people from outside the business are recruited.
Job advertised widely. — E.g. job centres, websites.

+ advert seen by more people — more likely to find right candidate

− expensive

Four Benefits of Good Recruitment

1. right skills and qualities → minimal training → **high productivity**
2. best skills → **high quality output**
3. well-suited to role and enjoying job → **good customer service**
4. well-suited to role → less likely to leave → **good staff retention**

Selection Process

Written Application
- Curriculum vitae (CV) — basic facts about the candidate and their skills or qualifications.
- Application form — all the info the firm needs and nothing else.

References
- Previous line manager provides statement about candidate's experience.

Interviews
- Same questions for everyone.
- Assess confidence, verbal skills, general attitude.
- Skills for a good interview are not always relevant to job.

Tests
- Might test ability, potential, personal qualities, teamwork.
- Assess skills relevant to job.

Section 4 — Human Resources

Staff Training

Induction Training

Induction training introduces a new employee to their workplace and helps them feel welcome.

It includes:
- introducing them to other workers
- explaining company rules and procedures
- initial training on their job

+ Advantages
- New employees feel confident.
- They are less likely to make mistakes — so they become productive quickly.
- They feel welcome and valued — so they're less likely to leave.

On-the-Job Training

On-the-job training is the most common type.

Employee learns by being shown how to do their job by more experienced colleagues and then practising.

E.g. learning how to use a till.

Most suitable for learning practical skills when it's safe and communication is easy.

+ Cost effective — employee works and learns at the same time.

− Training given by colleagues — bad working practices can be passed on.

− More expensive than on-the-job.

Off-the-Job Training

Employee learns away from their workplace — e.g. at a local college.

Most suitable for learning general information, such as skills not related to a specific task.

E.g. learning how to manage people.

+ High quality — taught by people qualified to train others.

Benefits of Training

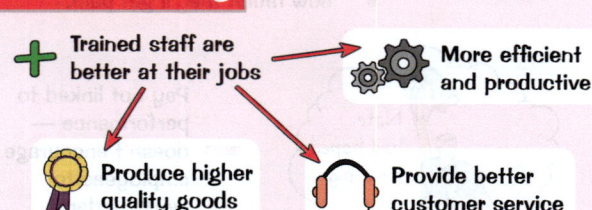

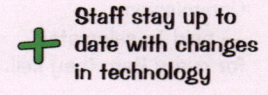

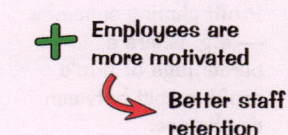

+ Trained staff are better at their jobs → More efficient and productive

Produce higher quality goods

Provide better customer service

+ Staff stay up to date with changes in technology

+ Employees are more motivated ↳ Better staff retention

Section 4 — Human Resources

Financial Motivation

Effect of Motivation

The more a worker is paid, the more motivated they are.

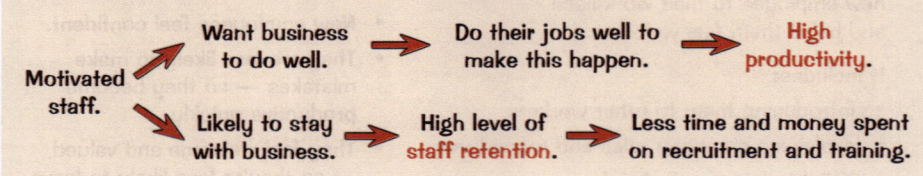

Motivated staff.
- → Want business to do well. → Do their jobs well to make this happen. → **High productivity**.
- → Likely to stay with business. → High level of **staff retention**. → Less time and money spent on recruitment and training.

Wages

- Paid weekly or monthly.
- Common for manual workers.

Time Rate — workers paid according to hours worked.

Best when measuring output is hard — e.g. driving a bus.

+ Encourages people to work long hours.

− Encourages people to work slowly.

Piece Rate — workers paid according to output.

Best when measuring output is easy — e.g. sewing garments.

+ Encourages people to work quickly.

− Working too quickly can reduce quality.

Salary

- A fixed amount paid every month.
- It doesn't change — even if the number of hours worked changes.
- Usually paid to office staff who don't directly help make the product.

+ Firm and workers know exactly how much they'll get paid.

− Pay not linked to performance — doesn't encourage employees to work harder.

Nate had hoped for a big salary.

Extra Payments

Some firms offer extra financial incentives — on top of the regular wage or salary.

Commission — paid to sales staff for every item they sell.

Profit sharing schemes — e.g. where a percentage of firm's profit is split between employees.

Section 4 — Human Resources

Non-Financial Motivation

Training

Knowledge and skills up to date. → Job performed well. → Increased self-esteem and job satisfaction. → More motivated.

Learning new skills means employees can take on new tasks and *greater responsibility*.

Employees less bored and more likely to stay with the firm. ← → Potential for promotion boosts motivation further.

Four Management Styles

1. **Authoritarian** (or autocratic) managers make decisions alone, without consulting staff.

   + Authoritarian management is effective at handling crises.
   − Can demotivate staff if they feel their views are not valued.

2. **Paternalistic** managers make decisions themselves, but after consultation with workers.

   A mix of management styles is often used — depending on the situation.

3. **Democratic** managers allow workforce some influence over decisions.

4. **Laissez-faire** managers allow workers to perform tasks as they see fit — offering help as needed.

Workers have input into decisions.
↓
They feel trusted and engaged with work.
↓
They are more motivated.

Fringe Benefits

FRINGE BENEFIT — any reward that is not part of a worker's main income.

Might include:
- staff discount on firm's products
- use of company car
- gym membership
- meal allowance
- health insurance

These *cost* money for the business and they *save* money for the worker.

Section 4 — Human Resources

The Marketing Mix

Four Elements to Marketing

1. Product
The product must fulfil customers' needs or wants.

2. Price
Customer must think the product is good value for money.

These four Ps make up the **marketing mix**.

3. Promotion
Potential customers need to know the product exists and want to buy it.

4. Place
Customers need to be able to buy the product — e.g. in a shop, online or straight from the producer.

Sandra was very pleased with her new marketing mix.

Different Marketing Mixes

The different elements of the marketing mix affect each other.

Some Ps are more important in certain situations than others.

Customers may pay a higher price if:
- they really want a product
- it's in a convenient place

Customers may pay a lower price if:
- they don't need a product
- it's not in a convenient place

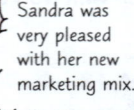

Adapting Over Time

Customers' needs change over time. Businesses should adapt their mix to match these needs.

Many products have changed over time from being physical to being digital.

The place where the products are bought has also changed (e.g. from a shop to a website).

Market Research

Structure of Markets

Businesses want to know the structure of a market.

1. **MARKET SHARE** — the proportion of total sales in the market controlled by a business.

2. **MARKET SIZE** — how many potential buyers or sellers of products there are, OR the total value of products in a market.

Market Segmentation

SEGMENTATION — when people within a market are divided into different groups.

Segmenting a market can help a business aim its marketing strategy at its...

TARGET MARKET — the specific group of people that a product is aimed at.

Four Ways to Segment a Market

1. **Age** — customers of different ages have different needs.

2. **Income** — how much money people earn affects what they will buy.

3. **Location** — people who live in different areas want different products.

4. **Gender** — products can be targeted towards, e.g. women or men.

Using Market Research

Market research helps firms understand its customers and competitors.

- It helps to create a good marketing mix.
- It identifies customers' needs — products are made that they want to buy.

Market research can stop companies from making costly mistakes (e.g. making too much of a product).

Three benefits of identifying these needs:

1. **Increase sales** — businesses can adjust pricing based on demand.

2. **Stay competitive** — gathering information shows differences between competitors, which can improve strategy.

3. **Create targeted marketing** — businesses can produce more effective promotional material and make relevant products for target market.

Section 5 — Marketing

More on Market Research

Market Opportunities

- A market opportunity is where customers have a need that isn't being met.
- There are four ways to meet customers' needs before competitors:

1. Develop a new product.
2. Sell an existing product in a new place.
3. Sell an existing product at a new price.
4. Promote the product differently.

Primary Market Research

PRIMARY RESEARCH — market research that involves getting information from customers or potential customers.

E.g. surveys, questionnaires, focus groups, interviews.

Advantages
- up-to-date information
- relevant and specific to a product
- can be targeted at specific markets

Disadvantages
- needs large samples to be reliable
- often expensive
- time-consuming

Secondary Market Research

SECONDARY RESEARCH — market research that involves looking at data collected by other people.

E.g. market reports, government reports, newspapers, internet research.

Advantages
- cheaper than primary research
- easily found
- instantly available

Disadvantages
- often out of date
- not always relevant
- not specific to firm's product

Types of Data

QUANTITATIVE DATA — information that can be measured or reduced to a number.

e.g. how many hours do you work a week?

QUALITATIVE DATA — information that involves people's feelings or opinions. It is hard to compare opinions, but they give a greater depth of information.

Good market research will contain both types of data.

Section 5 — Marketing

Product Life Cycles

Five Stages of Product Life Cycles

PRODUCT LIFE CYCLE — the different stages that a product goes through over time.

① Research and Development (R&D) — idea is developed and turned into a product. One aim is to find the most cost-effective way to make the product.

During R&D, big firms employ people who try to use scientific discoveries to develop new products.

② Introduction — product goes on sale. A lot of focus on promotion to increase demand.

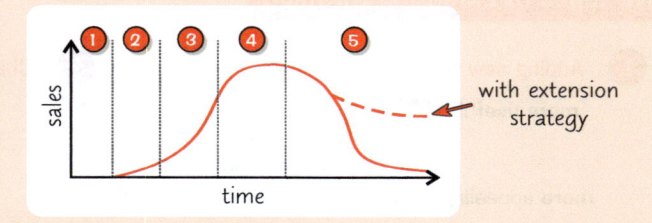

(graph: sales vs time, with stages ①②③④⑤ marked; dashed line labelled "with extension strategy")

③ Growth — demand for product increases and it becomes established.

④ Maturity — demand reaches peak. Firm focuses less on promotion and more on making product widely available, until market is saturated (there's no more room to expand).

⑤ Decline — demand falls as, e.g. rival products take over.

Profit and Loss During the Product Life Cycle

R&D and introduction — loss expected
Firm spends money on research and promotion, and sales will be low.

Growth and maturity — profit expected
Firm aims to make money back from initial investment and make a profit.

Decline — loss expected
Sales fall as firm spends less money on supporting the product.

Firms can reduce losses in the decline stage if they stop making the product.

Section 5 — Marketing

Extension Strategies

Extending the Life of a Product

EXTENSION STRATEGY — when a firm takes action to extend the life of a declining product.

If extension strategy works, product keeps selling and makes a profit for longer.

Firms need to find the right balance between spending money on extension strategies and developing new products.

Five Types of Extension Strategy

1. Adding new features
- more useful
- more appealing
→ increase in demand

2. Using new packaging
- more eye-catching
↓
customers more likely to see it

3. Changing target market
e.g. promote in a different age group or country

4. Changing advertising
↓
more people aware of product
↓
more appealing to new market

5. Lowering prices
e.g. reducing prices, or running special offers and competitions

Combining Extension Strategies

Some extension strategies are related to one another.

E.g. changing packaging or advertising will help to target a new market.

Businesses must evaluate the combination of strategies that will extend the life of their products.

Section 5 — Marketing

Product Portfolios

Range of Products

PRODUCT PORTFOLIO — range of different products a business sells.
Businesses want a balanced product portfolio. This includes:

1. a variety of different products
2. products at different stages of the life cycle

So if one product fails, they can still depend on others.

Piotr's fruit business did not have a balanced portfolio...

Four Product Types in a Boston Matrix

BOSTON MATRIX (or BOSTON BOX) — a way to analyse a business's product portfolio.

1. **Question marks** — low market share and high market growth. New products, so aren't profitable yet and need heavy marketing to succeed.

2. **Dogs** — low market share and growth. Mainly lost causes.

3. **Cash cows** — high market share and low market growth. Very profitable, costs are low and are produced in high volumes.

4. **Stars** — high market share and growth. Soon to be cash cows.

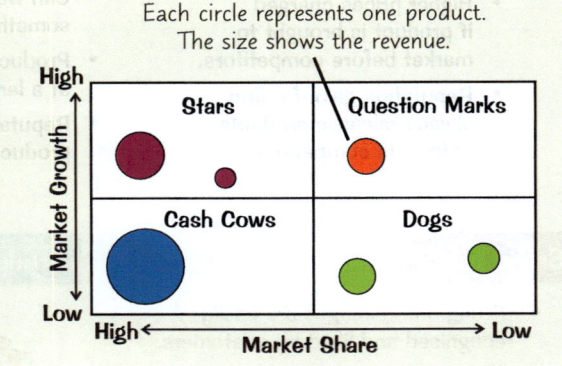

Each circle represents one product. The size shows the revenue.

(Boston Matrix diagram: Market Growth on y-axis (Low to High), Market Share on x-axis (High to Low). Quadrants: Stars (top-left), Question Marks (top-right), Cash Cows (bottom-left), Dogs (bottom-right).)

Using a Boston Matrix

+ Helps to see whether a business has a balanced product portfolio.

+ Identifies how to broaden a portfolio, e.g. not enough stars or cash cows.

− Can be misleading, e.g. a dog can still be profitable despite low market share.

Section 5 — Marketing

Product Development

Developing New Products

- High selling products eventually begin to decline.
- So businesses should have products in development and introduction stages.
- These grow to maturity and take place of the declining products.

Market-driven firms make new products from market research. Product-driven firms invent new things and try to sell them.

Benefits and Risks of Developing New Products

+ Benefits

- Increase in sales.
- May appeal to new market.
- Higher prices charged if product is brought to market before competitors.
- Reputation gain if a firm always releases products before its competitors.

− Risks

- Costly and time consuming if too much time spent in R&D.
- Can waste resources making something customers don't want.
- Product may not be able to be made at a large scale at a low enough cost.
- Reputation loss if new product is poor quality.

Brand Image

- **Strong brand images** are easily recognised and liked by customers.
- The marketing mix must be right to have a **positive brand image**.
- Gives a reputation for high quality, keeping customers loyal.

Firms spend many years and lots of money building a positive brand image.

Product Differentiation

- If a product isn't distinct, customers think it is identical to others.
- They have no reason to buy the product, unless it's cheaper.

UNIQUE SELLING POINT (USP) — a feature that makes the product different from competitors'.

Three factors of the **design mix** help with product differentiation.

1. **Function** — design is fit for purpose, can contain unique features.
2. **Cost** — good design will lead to low manufacturing costs.
3. **Appearance** — packaging can help a product stand out.

Section 5 — Marketing

Price

Price and Demand

DEMAND (for a product) — how much of the product customers are willing and able to buy.

As the price of a product rises, demand for it tends to fall.

Firms risk not selling many products if their prices are too high.

Demand at the bookshop was at an all time high.

Internal Factors Affecting Prices

1) Aims and objectives

If a business wants to:
- increase market share, it may lower its prices.
- expand, it might set prices to maximise profit to fund expansion.

2) Internal costs
- E.g. buying new machinery can reduce costs in the long term.
- Prices can then be reduced, but still return a profit.

3) Product life cycle

E.g. if the product is in the decline stage, the price may be lowered to increase demand again.

4) Changes to marketing mix

E.g. when promoting a product, prices may be reduced for a period.

External Factors Affecting Prices

1) Nature of the market

E.g. a luxury product can fetch a higher price than a similar, non-luxury product.

2) Competition
- Prices can't be much higher than competitors' prices.
- They also can't be much lower — customers will query the quality.

3) External costs

E.g. if costs of raw materials increase, prices may need to increase to make a profit.

> The size and age of the business also affect pricing. E.g. a larger, older firm might have loyal customers who are willing to pay slightly higher prices. They can also benefit from economies of scale to help keep prices down.

Section 5 — Marketing

Pricing Strategies

Price Penetration

Firm charges low price when product is new.

↓

Helps increase demand and establish market share.

↓

Once product is established, firm raises price to make more profit.

Loss Leader Pricing

Price of product is set below the cost of making it, so firm makes a loss on each sale.

Firm assumes that selling the product will increase sales of other, profitable products.

E.g. new games consoles are often sold at a loss, but the firm makes a profit on games bought for them.

Price Skimming

Firm charges high price when product is new as they know the demand will be high, e.g. because the firm has loyal customers or the product uses new, sought-after technology.

High price helps increase revenue and cover cost of development.

Firm lowers price once product is established to reach a wider market.

Competitive Pricing

Firm charges similar price to other firms. Usually happens if the market is very competitive and there isn't much differentiation.

Usually means little profit is made. Firm has to find ways other than price to attract customers, e.g. by providing good customer service.

A high price might also make the product more desirable to people with high incomes — this can improve the firm's image and status.

Cost-Plus Pricing

Firm decides price based on how much profit they want (while keeping demand high enough). Often happens when firm faces little price competition.

They could decide price by:

1 Using a mark-up — adding on a certain percentage to the cost of making the product.

2 Deciding on their desired profit margin and calculating the price required for it.

Section 5 — Marketing

Methods of Promotion

Four Reasons for Promoting a Product

Or remind customers about the product.

1. To **inform** — so customers know the product exists, its purpose and **USP**.

2. To **persuade** — firms tempt customers to choose their product over a competitor. Tactics can include displaying positive feedback and special offers.

3. To **create** or **change** the **image** — depending on who the product is aimed at.
E.g. humour and bold colours create a fun image, but darker colours used for a luxurious image.

4. To **create** or **increase sales** — more sales leads to more profit and market share.

Six Methods of Advertising

ADVERTISING — any message that a firm pays for to promote itself or its products.

1. **Newspapers**
Reach wide audience (national) or specific market (local), but poor print quality and falling reader numbers.

2. **Magazines**
Pricier than newspaper adverts, but better quality and targeted at specific interest groups.

3. **Posters/billboards**
Can be placed near a target audience and get seen often, but messages need to be short.

4. **Leaflets/flyers/business cards**
Cheap to produce and can be targeted at specific locations, but many people see them as junk.

5. **Television**
Can deliver longer message to wide audience, but very expensive.

6. **Internet**
Can reach wide and targeted audiences, and customers can click straight through to firm's website. But many people ignore or block them.

Sponsorship

SPONSORSHIP — when a firm gives money to an organisation or event in return for their name being displayed.

E.g. sports teams and competitions are often sponsored by firms.

World's Hottest Chilli Eating Championship — sponsored by Di's Dairy Farm.

+ can help raise firm's profile

− brand image can suffer if thing being sponsored gets bad publicity

Section 5 — Marketing

More Methods of Promotion

Six Methods of Promotion

1. Competitions
2. 2 for 1 offers
3. Free samples
4. Coupons
5. Point of sale displays
   E.g. branded display case at tills.
6. Free gifts

Public Relations (PR)

PUBLIC RELATIONS — activities that involve communicating with the media to promote a firm or its products to the public.
E.g. a TV interview or a press release.

+ PR is a cheap, easy way for a firm to get noticed by a wide audience.

− There's little control over how the media represents the firm — e.g. interviews can be edited.

+ Advantages
- encourages new customers to try product
- boosts sales in short term
- can boost sales in long term if new customers become loyal

− Disadvantages
- customers might not want to buy product when it's at full price
- might not be suitable for certain products (it makes it feel less of a luxury)

Social Media

Firms use social media to advertise products, offer sales promotions or share news to build excitement on new products.

+
- Can add information at any time.
- Customers can quickly navigate to a firm's website to buy product.

− Negative comments can be seen by loads of people, so firms must monitor sites.

Promotional Mix

PROMOTIONAL MIX — the combination of different promotional methods used to promote a product.

Factors that affect promotional mix:

- **Finance available** — large firms usually have more money to spend.

- **Nature of the product** — some products need detailed descriptions.

- **Competition** — firms may copy what their competitors are doing.

- **Target market** — promotions need to be seen by and appeal to the right people.

- **Nature of the market** — firms may spend more on rapidly growing markets.

Place

Channels of Distribution

CHANNEL OF DISTRIBUTION — the way products get from a manufacturer to a consumer.

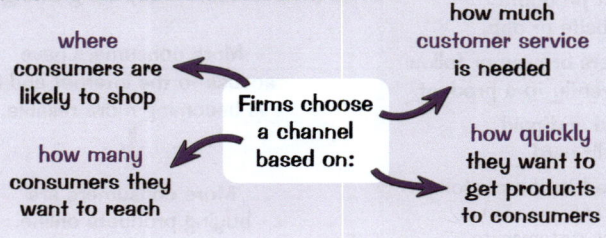

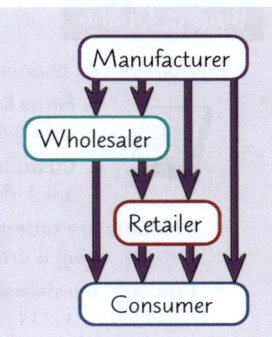

Firms choose a channel based on:
- where consumers are likely to shop
- how many consumers they want to reach
- how much customer service is needed
- how quickly they want to get products to consumers

Manufacturer → Wholesaler → Retailer → Consumer

Wholesalers

Manufacturers who make lots of a product often sell to wholesalers.

+ Advantages
- manufacturers don't need to store lots of stock
- wholesalers have existing customers, so products reach customers quickly
- retailers buy from wholesalers, reaching more customers

− Disadvantage
consumers may get low levels of customer service

Retailers

Manufacturers who sell to retailers can provide them with product knowledge.

+ Advantages
- good customer service, so high satisfaction with products
- retailers can promote products to increase sales
- products are sold in many places, exposing them to lots of potential customers

− Disadvantage
hard for new manufacturers to get retailers to stock their products

Telesales

Manufacturers who make one-off items or have few customers may use *telesales* — they sell products directly to consumers via phone.

+ Advantage
consumers may get a better price than buying from a wholesaler or retailer

− Disadvantages
- time-consuming to sell to individuals
- expensive to arrange delivery of goods

Section 5 — Marketing

E-Commerce

Buying Online

Customers can choose to buy online.

- Firms list products on a website or app.
- Customers browse or follow a link directly to a product.
- Products are ordered and paid for, e.g. using a credit card.
- Products are delivered to the customer.

Smartphones allow customers to shop online wherever they are.

Growth of E-Commerce

E-commerce and **m-commerce** (mobile commerce) are growing fast.

More consumers have access to the internet and it is becoming more reliable.

⬇

More consumers are buying products online.

⬇

Businesses must adapt to keep up with changing **expectations** and **competition**.

Customers expect:
- to be able to buy from a firm online
- low prices
- free delivery and returns
- an easy-to-use website

Customers are able to:
- buy from firms around the world
- easily compare products and prices on different websites

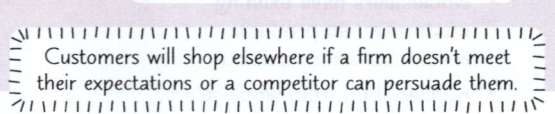

Customers will shop elsewhere if a firm doesn't meet their expectations or a competitor can persuade them.

Reasons for Using E-Commerce

➕ Advantages

- easy access to international markets — more potential customers, so sales may increase
- saves money on printing
- reduced staff and property costs if high street shops close
- can relocate offices to cheaper areas with lower wages
- savings mean lower prices can be offered than a high street shop

It's also cheaper to do online promotions for overseas markets than advertise in foreign newspapers, etc.

➖ Disadvantages

- equipment needs to be bought and installed
- specialist website or app designers need to be employed
- staff need training in using equipment to provide good customer service
- some consumers are reluctant to buy online and prefer shopping in person

Section 5 — Marketing

Section 6 — Finance

Sources of Finance

Five Reasons New or Small Businesses Need Finance

1. Start-up capital to set up the business.
2. To cover poor initial cash flow.
3. To cover a shortfall in cash, e.g. because of delayed payments from customers.
4. To cover day-to-day running costs of struggling businesses.
5. To expand the business, e.g. to pay for new premises or equipment.

Government Grants

- Grants are typically given to new or small firms.
- They do not have to be repaid.
- Strict criteria needed for firms to qualify.
- May have to spend money in a specific way.

Long-Term Sources

Three types of loans:

1. Bank loans
- **+** Quick and easy, lower interest rates than overdrafts.
- **−** Bank can repossess assets if not repaid.

2. Friends and family
- **+** Money goes into firm immediately.
- **−** Lender may expect a share in profits.

3. Mortgages — used to finance property.
- **+** Interest is low.
- **−** Property used as collateral.

Banks can take property if payments aren't made.

Short-Term Sources

Trade credit — paying suppliers one or two months after the purchase.
- **+** time to earn money to repay debt
- **−** late repayment = large fees

Overdrafts — taking more money out of a bank account than is actually in it.
- **+** can make payments on time without having the cash
- **−** high interest rate, bank can cancel overdraft, bank can repossess assets if not paid back

If only Kyle had repaid his overdraft, he would still have his favourite hat.

Hire purchase — deposit paid and rest is paid in instalments over time.
- Firm has long-term use of a product.
- Can use a product they couldn't otherwise afford.

Long-term sources are good for a firm's cash flow.

Section 6 — Finance

More Sources of Finance

Three Sources for Established Firms

1) RETAINED PROFITS — profits that are put back into the firm.
- Owners reinvest profits after dividends paid.
- Larger companies give large dividends to shareholders.

Established firms are less likely to go bankrupt, so are less risky for banks to lend money to.

2) FIXED ASSETS — assets that a business keeps long-term, e.g. machinery or buildings.
- Fixed assets that aren't being used can be sold.
- Limit to how much can be sold — some are needed to keep trading.

3) NEW SHARE ISSUES — money raised through selling new shares.
- Only an option for limited companies.
- Money raised doesn't need to be repaid.
- More shareholders means less control for existing owners.

Internal and External Finance

Retained profits, Selling fixed assets → **INTERNAL FINANCE** — from inside the firm.

Personal/business savings →

Government grants, New share issues, Hire purchase, Loans, overdrafts and mortgages, Trade credit → **EXTERNAL FINANCE** — from outside the firm.

Four Factors Affecting Choice

1) Size and type of business
Not all firms can access all types of finance. Some firms have no fixed assets or cannot issue new shares.

2) Duration of finance
E.g. savings or overdraft useful to cover for short lengths of time.

3) Amount of money needed
- Small amounts from internal.
- Large amounts from external.

4) Cost of the finance
Some sources are more expensive than others, e.g. bank loans and overdrafts.

Section 6 — Finance

Investments

Investment Projects

INVESTMENT — money put into a business to make improvements that make the business more profitable. Three examples are:

1) New machinery
- able to make new products
- more efficient processes

2) New buildings
- increase number of employees
- increase amount of machinery
- increase amount of stock held

3) New vehicles
- more vehicles
- larger vehicles

Good for businesses that offer delivery services.

Arasha's new food delivery service was a hole-in-one...

Average Rate of Return

RETURN ON INVESTMENT — how much a business makes or loses as a proportion of the original money put in.

AVERAGE RATE OF RETURN (ARR) — the average return on an investment each year over its lifespan.

Two steps to calculate ARR:

1) Work out the average annual profit.

$$\text{average annual profit} = \frac{\text{total profit}}{\text{number of years}}$$

2) Use the formula to find ARR.

$$\text{ARR (\%)} = \frac{\text{average annual profit}}{\text{cost of investment}} \times 100$$

EXAMPLE

The table below shows the profit made by a business on a £2m investment over three years. Calculate the average rate of return for the investment.

	Profit (£)
Year 1	70 000
Year 2	95 000
Year 3	105 000

1) average annual profit = $\frac{\text{total profit}}{\text{number of years}}$ = $\frac{70\,000 + 95\,000 + 105\,000}{3}$
= 270 000 ÷ 3 = £90 000

2) average rate of return = $\frac{\text{average annual profit}}{\text{cost of investment}} \times 100$ = $\frac{90\,000}{2\,000\,000} \times 100$
= 0.045 × 100 = **4.5%**

Section 6 — Finance

Break-Even Analysis

Break-Even Output

BREAK-EVEN OUTPUT — the level of output a business needs to cover its costs.

Selling more than break-even output = profit.
Selling less than break-even output = loss.

New businesses should do a **break-even analysis** to find the break-even output.

A low break-even output means a business doesn't have to sell as much to make a profit.

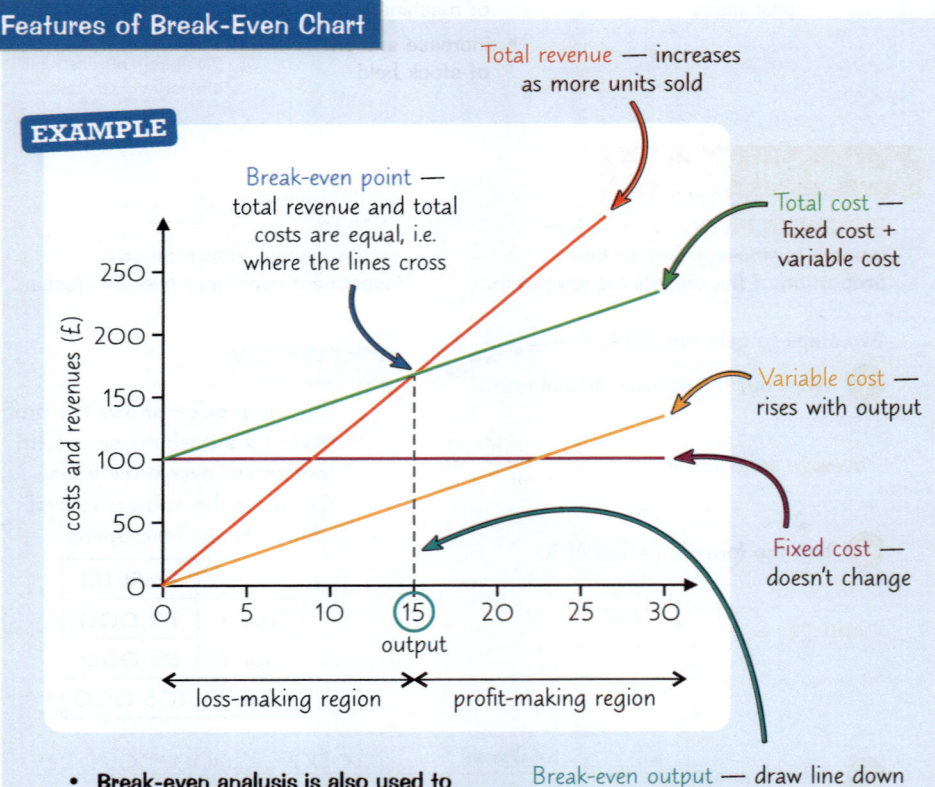

Features of Break-Even Chart

EXAMPLE

- Total revenue — increases as more units sold
- Break-even point — total revenue and total costs are equal, i.e. where the lines cross
- Total cost — fixed cost + variable cost
- Variable cost — rises with output
- Fixed cost — doesn't change

(Graph: costs and revenues (£) on y-axis from 0 to 250; output on x-axis from 0 to 30. Break-even point at output = 15. Loss-making region to the left, profit-making region to the right.)

- Break-even output — draw line down from break-even point to output axis
- In this example, the break-even output is 15 units.

• Break-even analysis is also used to see the effect of changing output.
• In example above, total cost is rising slower than total revenue.
• This means an increase in **profit per unit** for every unit output.

Section 6 — Finance

More on Break-Even Analysis

Margin of Safety

MARGIN OF SAFETY — how much a business's output can fall before a loss is made.

You can show the margin of safety on a break-even chart.

EXAMPLE

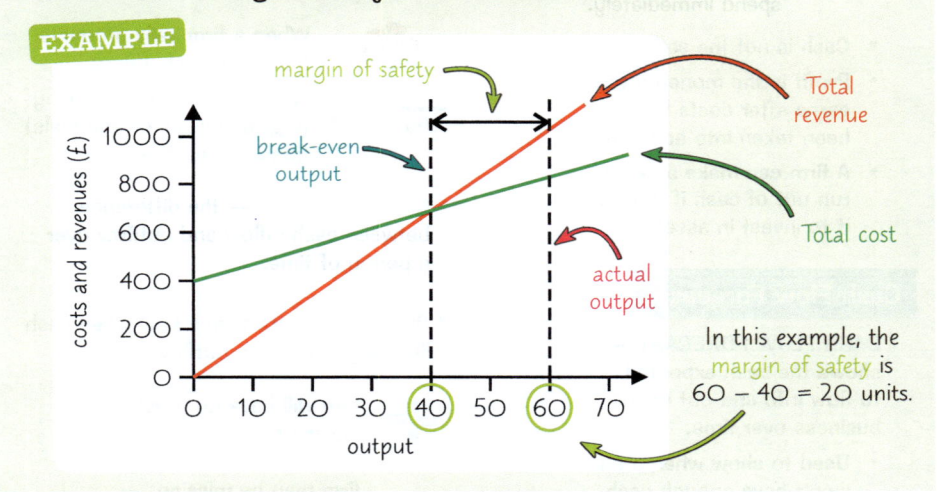

(Break-even chart showing costs and revenues (£) on y-axis from 0 to 1000, output on x-axis from 0 to 70. Labels: margin of safety, break-even output, actual output, Total revenue, Total cost. Break-even at 40, actual output at 60.)

In this example, the margin of safety is 60 − 40 = 20 units.

Five Advantages of Analysis

1.  Easy to work out.
2.  It's quick to make. Immediate action can be taken to increase sales or reduce costs.
3.  Helps predict how changes in sales affect revenue.
4.  Used to convince banks to give loans.
5.  Stops releasing products that are difficult to sell in large quantities.

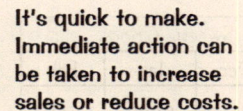

Five Disadvantages of Analysis

1.  Assumes any quantity of product can be sold at current price.
2.  Assumes all products are sold without waste.
3. 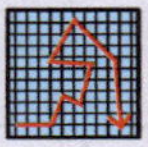 Wrong results if data is wrong.
4.  Complicated if more than one product is involved.
5.  Only shows what a firm needs to sell, not what it will sell.

Section 6 — Finance

Cash Flow

Cash and Profit

CASH — the money that a business can spend immediately.

- Cash is not the same as profit.
- Profit is the money a firm earns after costs have been taken into account.
- A firm can make a profit but run out of cash if it uses it to invest in assets.

Cash Flow Forecasts

CASH FLOW FORECAST — shows the cash expected to flow into and out of the business over time.

- Used to show when a business won't have enough cash.
- Can see when a short-term finance, e.g. an overdraft, may be needed.
- Should be watched carefully to monitor impact of unexpected cash flows.

Net Cash Flow

CASH FLOW — the flow of money into and out of a business.

When a firm sells products there is a cash inflow.

When a firm spends money (e.g. on wages or materials) there is a cash outflow.

NET CASH FLOW — the difference between cash inflow and outflow over a period of time.

A firm has a positive cash flow when cash inflow is greater than outflow.

+ firm will have no problem making payments

− firm may be missing opportunities to invest

A business can make an overall profit even if it has a poor cash flow.

Moving into Tuesday evening, it's going to be raining cash...

Cash Flow Forecast — Sweetie Chocs	Dec	Jan	Feb
Total receipts (cash inflow)	7000	800	5500
Total payments (cash outflow)	4500	4500	4000
Net cash flow (inflow − outflow)	2500	(3700)	1500
Opening balance (bank balance at start of month)	1000	3500	(200)
Closing balance (bank balance at end of month)	3500	(200)	1300

Net cash flow is negative in January — outflow is greater than inflow.

Numbers in brackets are negative.

Opening balance = closing balance of previous month

Closing balance = opening balance + net cash flow

They will need extra finance in January — knowing this in advance means they can plan ahead.

Section 6 — Finance

More on Cash Flow

Three Effects of Poor Cash Flow

A poor cash flow means there isn't enough cash for day-to-day expenses.

Effects on a business include:

> Credit terms tell a customer how long they have until they need to pay for a product.

1 staff not paid on time → resentment and poor motivation

2 creditors not paid on time → may insist on stricter credit terms or take legal action

3 can't take advantage of discounts offered by suppliers for prompt payments

Three Reasons for Poor Cash Flow

1 Poor sales
- Lack of demand from the consumers for products.
- Less money coming in.

2 Overtrading
- Firm takes on too many orders so buys lots of raw materials.
- Issue with orders means firm doesn't get money from customers quickly enough to pay debts.

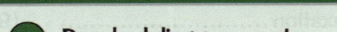

3 Poor business decisions
- Firm brings out new products in new markets that don't bring in as much money as forecast.

Five Ways to Improve Cash Flow

1 Rescheduling payments
- Give customers less generous credit terms.
- Negotiate better credit terms with suppliers.

2 Reducing cash outflow
- Firms may carry a stock of unsold products.
- These could be sold instead of making more.

3 Arranging an overdraft

4 Finding new finance sources — E.g. a new business partner

5 Increasing cash inflow — E.g. by increasing selling price

Section 6 — Finance

Income Statements

Three Parts to Income Statements

INCOME STATEMENT — statement that shows how income has changed over time.

① The trading account — records gross profit or loss over a period of time.

- **Revenue** — the value of all products sold.
- **Cost of sales** — how much the products cost to make (the direct costs).

cost of sales = (opening stock + purchases) − closing stock

gross profit = revenue − cost of sales

② The profit and loss account — records indirect costs of running the business.

- Covers the cost of **depreciation** (amount of value an asset has lost).
- Money left after indirect costs (**expenses**) is the **operating profit**.
- After interest paid (or received) is included, **net profit** is left over.

③ The appropriation account — records where the profit has gone.

```
Income Statement
Superb Sofas Ltd.
Year ending 31st March 2024
```
means numbers shown are in the thousands → £000 £000

Revenue....................		250
Cost of sales:		
Opening stock....	5	
Purchases..........	45	
	50	
Minus closing stock....	(4)	
Cost of sales = ...		(46)
Gross profit = ...		204
Minus expenses		
Wages and salaries..	108	
Rents and rates......	16	
Office expenses......	10	
Advertising.............	11	
Depreciation...........	9	
Other expenses........	2	
Expenses = ...		(156)
Operating profit = ...		48
Interest payable		(2)
Profit before tax (Net profit)		46
Taxation		(9)
Dividends		(18)
Retained profit....................		19

Business Performance from Income Statement Values

Gross profit — if it is low then ways of increasing revenue or reducing costs should be explored to make gross profit higher.

Operating profit — weak area if it is significantly lower than gross profit. If it is too low, banks will be reluctant to invest.

Retained profit — shows profitability of a firm. A larger retained profit shows the business has potential to get bigger.

Profit Margins

Gross Profit Margin

GROSS PROFIT MARGIN — the fraction of every pound spent by customers that doesn't go directly towards making a product.

$$\text{gross profit margin} = \frac{\text{gross profit}}{\text{revenue}} \times 100$$

Can be improved by:

↑ increasing price

↓ reducing cost of making product

Higher gross profit margin is better, but what counts as a 'good' profit margin depends on the type of business.

E.g. supermarkets have low gross profit margins because they keep prices low to compete, but can still make large profits as they sell in high volumes.

EXAMPLE

In one year, Polly's Paper made a gross profit of £72 000 from a revenue of £180 000. Calculate the gross profit margin.

gross profit margin

$$= \frac{\text{gross profit}}{\text{revenue}} \times 100$$

$$= \frac{72\,000}{180\,000} \times 100$$

$$= 0.4 \times 100 = 40\%$$

This means for every £1 spent by customers, 60p was used to make the product, leaving 40p.

In the same year, Polly's Paper had operating expenses of £42 000 and paid £3000 of interest on loans. Calculate the net profit margin.

First work out the net profit.

net profit = gross profit − (operating expenses + interest)
= 72 000 − (42 000 + 3000)
= 72 000 − 45 000 = £27 000

$$\text{net profit margin} = \frac{\text{net profit}}{\text{revenue}} \times 100$$

$$= \frac{27\,000}{180\,000} \times 100$$

$$= 0.15 \times 100 = 15\%$$

This means for every £1 spent by customers, 15p is kept by the business as net profit.

Net Profit Margin

NET PROFIT MARGIN — the fraction of every pound spent by customers that the business keeps as net profit.

$$\text{net profit margin} = \frac{\text{net profit}}{\text{revenue}} \times 100$$

Like for gross profit margin, higher net profit margin is better, but what counts as a 'good' margin depends on the business.

Net profit margin can decrease as a firm grows and has more costs (e.g. more salaries, more spent on rent or utilities).

Section 6 — Finance

Statements of Financial Position

Fixed Assets

STATEMENT OF FINANCIAL POSITION — shows where a business got its money from and what's been done with it.

A business uses some money to buy **fixed assets**.

The total figure shown is what they're worth on the date of the statement.

The first part of a statement of financial position shows what has been done with the money.

Current Assets

Current assets — listed from least to most liquid.

Liquidity is how easily assets can be converted into money.

- **Stock** — raw materials and finished products that have not been sold.
- **Debtors** — sold products that haven't been paid for by customers yet.
- **Cash** — money that hasn't been spent yet.

Current Liabilities

Payments that have to be made within a year of the date on the statement.

- **Creditors** — money that the firm owes to suppliers.
- **Corporation tax** — payable to government out of the year's profit.

Net Assets

NET CURRENT ASSETS — money available for day-to-day operations. Also known as **working capital**.

Can be worked out by subtracting the current liabilities from the current assets.

NET ASSETS — what the business is worth (if it sold all its assets). *Also known as 'net worth'.*

Can be worked out by adding fixed assets to net current assets.

EXAMPLE

Statement of Financial Position
Polly's Pizza Ltd., 31st March 2024

	£000	£000
Fixed assets		
Premises		60
Machinery		20
Vehicles		30
		110
Current assets		
Stock	5	
Debtors	15	
Cash	7	
	27	
Current liabilities		
Creditors	(21)	
Corporation tax	(2)	
	(23)	
Net current assets		4
Net assets		114
Financed by		
Shareholders' funds		
Share capital		65
Retained profit		20
Long-term liabilities		
Bank loan		21
Mortgage		8
Capital employed		114

Section 6 — Finance

More on Statements of Financial Position

Two Parts to Shareholders' Funds

The second part of a statement of financial position is where all the money came from.

EXAMPLE

Financed by	
Shareholders' funds	
Share capital	65
Retained profit	20
Long-term liabilities	
Bank loan	21
Mortgage	8
Capital employed	114

1) Share capital
- Money put into the business when shares were originally issued.
- Not the same as what shares are currently worth.
- Firms can raise new capital by issuing new shares.

Can be done through a rights issue, where existing shareholders are offered new shares at reduced prices.

2) Retained profits and reserves
- Profit the firm has made over the years that it has kept instead of paying out dividends.
- Profit is retained to finance future investment and to protect against future problems.
- Falls under the shareholders' funds as profits are really their money — it's just been left in the firm.

"Wait, are you trying to tell me money doesn't grow on trees..."

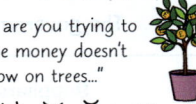

Long-Term Liabilities
- Firms also get money from sources other than shareholders.
- Any debts that will take more than a year to repay are **long-term liabilities**.

Not the same as current liabilities.

Capital Employed

The **capital employed** accounts for all the firm's sources of money.

capital employed = shareholders' funds + long-term liabilities

Money the firm got (capital employed) must be equal to what the firm has done with that money (net assets).

Capital employed is equal to net assets.

Section 6 — Finance

Analysis of Financial Statements

Uses of Statements of Financial Position

Statements of financial position can:

- be used to assess a firm's performance at a point in time.
- show sources of capital.
- be used to work out working capital and liquidity.

A firm can use its working capital and liquidity to help make business decisions.

Three Trends Over Time

Statements of financial position can be compared over a number of consecutive years.

Three things to compare are:

1. **Fixed assets** — a quick increase implies business has invested.
2. **Retained profits** — increase suggests an increase in profits.
3. **Liabilities** — amount and types show how well-managed a firm is.

Five Stakeholders Interested in Financial Analysis

	Stakeholder	Why they assess the statement
1	Existing shareholders	To see if directors are making sensible decisions.
2	Potential shareholders or lenders	May consider investing if the business is making lots of profit.
3	Employees	They may get a pay rise if the business is profitable.
4	The government	To see how much tax a business owes.
5	Suppliers	Higher liquidity means firm is more likely to pay bills on time.

Comparing Financial Statements of Competitors

- Income statements can be used to compare revenue, expenses and profit.
- Statements of financial position can compare each firm's worth and their liabilities.
- Some firms are hard to compare as they can operate in different ways. Direct comparison can be done by calculating gross and net profit margins.

Section 6 — Finance